To Gail

Best Wishes

[signature]

About the Author

Muriel Garcia was born and educated in Cardiff. During her long working life she held a variety of posts. These included working in a library, joining the WRNS and teaching. Latterly, until retirement, she became a verger in a large parish church. Her time now is spent walking, listening to music and writing poetry.

In memory of Christine Best
A Director of Music, who inspired so many old and young.

Muriel Garcia

A MAN OF MANY PARTS AND OTHER VERSES

AUSTIN MACAULEY
PUBLISHERS LTD.

A CIP catalogue record for this title is available from the British Library.

ISBN 978 1 78455 761 4 (Paperback)
ISBN 978 1 78455 759 1 (Hardback)

www.austinmacauley.com

First Published (2015)
Austin Macauley Publishers Ltd.
25 Canada Square
Canary Wharf
London
E14 5LB

Printed and bound in Great Britain

Acknowledgments

Certainly this collection of poems came about due to the environment I lived in, so I should like to thank my late husband Ronald and of course all who trod my paths during its writings.

Contents

A Man of Many Parts

Once a ball of bouncing flesh.
He never would stay in his crèche;
With such a jolly point of view,
He smiled at everyone he knew.

As life proceeded
He succeeded
To stretch his bounce to brawn.

As years went by
With Pop and Trad
No longer such a growing lad.

Instead of pop
Instead of bounce
Of flesh he has but half an ounce.

He daily rushes in and out,
To his office where there's doubt
About the brightness of the staff.

Because he has to make them laugh.

Now he's on a different track
Because he's had to learn the knack
Of turning brawn into a brain,
And studying on a different plane.

Should you meet him,
In years to come
He will be having,
Oh, such fun!

Whilst not bouncing,
He'll be announcing
Everything, that is to come.

I .T.

Instead of an email
You may have a ring.
Instead of a ring
I better sing.

Instead of torture,
It's better to wait
Than risk a misfortune
I'd rather state –
Happy Christmas.

To a candle (from a penknife)

Would you like a flourishing flame?
For I can achieve the very same.
Are you ashamed of your ruffled collar?
Allow me to use my blade
Like a scholar.

If you've disgraced yourself with a trickle
Feel my swift action without a prickle.
Soon your wick will be so proud,
With all the attention you've allowed.

When in place,
Those down the aisle,
Will surely return your beaming smile.
At last you will glow up on high,
In line with others in the sky.

The Room

The walls are plain
In every way.
To touch is to feel a strain
Of worry, sadness and disdain.

Strike up a glow
Of golden red
To lighten every thread
Of sorrow borne.

In solitude and meditation,
You sit alone
As if upon a lonely throne.

Let not this whisper
'Ere again
Lest it should become reframed.

In joyous colour
Print and cord.
You'll see the room
You can accord.

To be your domiciliary cave
Where everything is there to save.

The Rabbit

The rabbit has a pleasant face,
His private life is a disgrace.
I really could not tell to you
The awful things a rabbit can do.

Secretly he taps away
Deep in his furrowed hideaway.
He slowly gathers up the spoil,
He's stolen, and tries to foil.

Listen though, the others hear
With long and pointed furry ear.
What he's up to they all know.
He's taken someone else's doe.

Not for long does he carry on,
As the crime rabbit comes along
To see who else he's pilfered from.
To put a stop to what is wrong.

What to do, poor rabbit thinks,
People start to say "I stink".
Well at last he has to crumble in
His internet, to repent of sin.

Rabbit has a pleasant face
But now he's simply in disgrace.
He's burrowing hard to make it right,
To mend the damage done in spite.

At Eighteen

Now you are a Miss
Remember this.
Make friends with the truth.
Shed all that is idle,
Stare reality in the face,
And, "D'you know what"?
You are sure to find
Grace.

At Nineteen

Sincere, true Nature,
Fills your purpose.

Try, try again,
It's not in vain.

Be still and strong
For ever long,
Wait, increase the wonder,
Uphold the marvel.
True nature fills your purpose,
Peace perfects the picture.

The Mystery

Say it with music,
Say it with song.
Why wait to say it?
It's here all along.

In far off places
Or even next door.
In wide open spaces
It's there to be sure.

It's there in the trees,
As they sway to and fro
And whisper and rustle
In time with the breeze.

Voices rise high over trees,
While crows protest from their nests.
The errand boy whistles as he cycles –
With ease.
Wearing his Sunday best.

Its magic, its beauty.
It fills us with tears.
But when it is hostile
Its silence brings fears.

How can we measure its invisible force
Which natures' concerts provide?
How can we find its extraordinary source,
That no one will truly confide?

Listen, oh listen to the audition
That surrounds us all the day.
Be thankful and listen
In case – it fades away.

I am

I am a bulbous creature,
With no redeeming feature.
Just try me out
When you are about –
I am your friend!

I need so little feeding.
I pick up every seedling.
Dirty morsels are my delight,
I swallow everything in sight.

I love to run,
I have such fun,
When doing all I can,
To leave you spick and span.

So when you need me
I'm ready really
To give a helping hand
You understand

Your friend.

Bells

When times stands still at every peal,
Revolving distance like a wheel.
Your heart engages with a thrill,
Mixed with moments of anguish still.

Unrolling fragments of hazy dreams,
Of happenings vague and without seams
Of threads so fragile as to be lost.
Entangled plaits quite firmly tossed.

Memories that can never fail
To touch the soul and bring a hail
Of tears, and melancholy flavour.
Life requires it by our saviour.

But bells so faintly lose their sound,
And we take on some fresher ground.
The joyful message of their tune,
Replaces all the sadness soon.

For there will be another peel,
To bring together and to seal.
By rings of joy and rings of love,
Arranged in union from above.

Simon

Serenity,
Love, dreams,
Eyes wide with wonder.

Tenderness,
Brings more love,
Such wonder
Calls of welcome.

Love's spirit
Joins the circle.

Joy
Gently prospers.

Lie still
Delicate and strong
Wait.
Increase the wonder
Uphold the marvel.
Sincere, true
Nature
Fills your purpose.

Lie still
Peace
Perfects – the picture.

Untitled No.3

Chance the unfamiliar,
Unwind mysterious lanes,
Tread the awkward carpets
Of twigs and tangled canes.
For thereby lies the secrets
Of life's eternal gains.

Search the untaught talents
Unharness things of nought.
For shade obscures the beauty
Of which sincerity is part.

Then waiting will enhance,
And provide
Wisdom to the worthy pilgrim
And chance
To witness life's excitement,
Its mystery, its charm.

Untitled No.4

Untie my scarf
Lest I become
Reduced by half.

I have no belt
No wish to melt.
So hurry now
And find out
How –
To prise me open
Before I'm broken.

For once untied,
I must confide
There's more to hide.
No, not a cube of frozen snow,
Nor a tube of playing dough.

Just take a guess
Lest I confess,
To what's inside.

And spoil the fun
Yet not – undone.

The Bottle

Though this something of a flask,
'Tis more a festive dose.
To sup from it, 'tis just a mask,
To discover your vivacity.

Take a gentle measure
As may be your pleasure.

Harmonise in benevolence,
Spare no reverence
Then pause –

With sparkling eyes
You'll see eye to eye
Your future
Where perception lies.

From now on

Today is for leisure
To indulge in pleasure.
Turn the pages of yesteryear,
Remembering all that which is dear,
But, the passage of time has led you here
Upon a new plateau.

Here you'll see a fresher view,
Surprising and wholly new.
An unfamiliar perspective,
Gaze and be reflective.
From your plateau.

So pour a full measure.
Celebrate with pleasure with your glasses raised,
To fun be praised.
Relaxing on your plateau.

So long gone

Where are you now my darling boy?
So long gone.
Can you see me writing this?
And do you know how much I miss
Our being in such tremendous bliss?
So long gone.

Take a day and then another
To try my best to recover,
From losing my beloved.
You slipped away without a word,
And floated to a better world.
So long gone.

I see you sitting in your chair
It really is too much to bear.
So long gone.

Tomorrow will be one more day
Without my lover.
So long gone.
Yet I pray the time
Will pass away
So swiftly – you've not long gone.

The Walk

The only sign there was to guide
(Our path was most obscure
For twigs, and nettles all entwined)
An arch of oaks mature.

With vigilance we plodded
On roughness so unsound.
Whilst above, the branches nodded,
To keep going we were bound.

The corridor of greenness
Began to fade away.
The shade gave way to brightness,
The sun began to play.

Dwindling thicket, patchy stubble
Eased the way beneath our feet.
Clumps of moss replaced the rubble,
Ahead, we faced a field of wheat.

A stunning scene of ripe perfection,
Quelled our minds of any fear.
A rotten post displayed direction.
At last our route was clear.

A Wish

I wish I had a pony and trap,
To take me out in the evening.
We'd watch the bird's rabbit and hare.
And rattle along without a care.

I wish I had a speed boat.
I'd never need to wear a coat.
Or use the paddles or the oars,
Just as well; they're left indoors.

I wish I had a magic wand,
I'd float across every pond,
Ski down every piste,
Yet still land upon my feet.

Every child could learn to read
With an increasing speed.
Better still to write with ease
Sufficient for the parents to please.

Then a last wave of this magic,
To waste its power would be tragic.
To instil in many, common sense.
Better still, at no expense!
Ah – I wish.

The Music Man – The Encore

From a quayside tiny billet,
A lonesome figure in tattered gilet
Strolls along the harbour wall.
Enclosing craft large and small.

No stranger to the local scene,
His life has always been
A solitary one;
Except for Mog
His friendly furry sheepdog.

If by chance you walk around
The ancient square of this old town
No doubt you'd hear a distant sound.
A melodeon, so well known.

Wander on towards the tune
Till there, before you very soon,
Sits a hunchback in baggy cords
His hands outstretched upon the boards.

The instrument is very old
Worth far too much so I am told.
His fingers nimble on the keys,
Produced some lovely melodies.

An audience is always there,
To listen with the utmost care.
They love the old familiar lyrics
Which raise the eyebrows of some critics.

Mog sprawls out upon the floor
And is careful where he puts his paw.
Gently resting it upon the can
Which holds the takings of the music man.

He watches all around the square,
Of any strangers, he is well aware
Although his eyes are deeply set
He has never missed a prowler yet.

The music continues for a while,
In a rhythmic and jolly style.
And suddenly before their eyes
The audience is taken by surprise.

Alas, the melodeon is quickly seized,
The music man is most displeased.
A chase begins and off they go
In pursuit of an audacious foe.

At last they catch up with the thief,
Who is shocked and shaking like a leaf.
Mog jumps up and holds him firmly
Whilst his master speaks to him most sternly.

Such excitement marks the day.
A policeman hustles the thief away.
Mog, the audience and many more
Are delighted with the most unusual – encore.

The Geranium Basket

In the quiet and stillness of the day,
Some special visitors came our way.
We had no plans to entertain,
We had a reputation to maintain.

At first, just two or three arrived
No wonder we were surprised,
When dozens found their way indoors
Gathering everywhere, except the floors.

Jumping up and down with vigour
It would certainly improve our figure.
We did our best to obliterate
Those arriving at a frightening rate.

The ceiling that once was white,
Had now become a different site
A covering of buzzing flies
Was all we saw before our eyes.

Flipping, flicking, swiping and swatting,
Twisting and turning, and even squatting,
Our assault and efforts all in vain
Because the numbers remained the same.

Then at last we tried a spray
Hoping it would be the way
To finally defeat our foe
And put an end to the show.

Into the garden by force we sprung
To the spot where the hose was hung.
And inspiration had come about:
A more powerful spray would root them out.

The direction of the friendly hose
Did more than we did propose
The geranium basket hanging near
Accidentally, was the subject of our fear.

Success at last,
And we could rest
Our guests dispersed towards the west.
Relief and humour filled the air,
Our ceiling now was completely bare.

Our friends were staying right next door,
And thought they might like to explore.
That is how it came about,
They had such fun going in and out.

Our visitors are no longer
From their nest expelled,
We the stronger.
Flies galore no more; not one.
"Let us go and sit in the sun."

Christmas

See the line in winter
So idle and forlorn.
No shawl, no robe or singlet
Bedecks its lonely form.

See the line in winter,
Waiting for the sun
To dry its unhung garments
All soaked and tightly wrung.

See the line in winter,
When frost and ice appear
Strung gently twixt the hedges
A path from which to peer.

See the line in winter
When it begins to sway.
And forms a secret entrance
A blue tit's right of way.

See the line in winter
No longer obsolete.
Two tiny birds hop gently,
Towards their country seat.

See the line in winter
Does not hang there in vain.
For those who plan their future,
Make use of this terrain.

From this line in winter
They survey their hiding place.
In readiness for spring time
Their old haunt they will retrace.

Therefore the line in winter
Provides a hopeful song,
Foretells a joyful message,
From –
A twittering, tiny, throng.

The Host

'Tis worth a million smiles,
A mile of golden isles,
In the presence
Of our host.

In between four walls,
Top of many floors,
There dines our
Perfect host.

No need for chandeliers
Or for a buckled peer
With our sincere
Host.

We talk with ease,
A little tease,
No prompting from
Our host.

The food is fine
As is the wine,
But then, he is
The perfect host.

Still in a dream
And tastes of cream.
Can you believe
We had to leave
A very proper,
Host?

Bubble and Squeak

As soon as the sun begins to shine,
This pair will surely find the time
To bathe within its rays.

Abundant fur of mostly black
With specks of white upon their back.
They're round balloons of fluff.

Each day these sisters do the rounds,
To seek out any moving sounds.
Their tool of trade is – patience.

At other times they find a spot
To lay stretched out if it is hot.
Their lives are full of leisure.

If they should have a thirst for knowledge,
They sightsee from a window ledge.
Curiosity is a blessing.

Both love the life of pleasure.
At night they hunt for treasure.
'Tis Nature's ingenuity!

Bubble and Squeak are a queenly pair,
With nothing more than time to spare.
With nine lives – what do they care?

Binoculars

In the stillness of the night,
I focus upon a heavenly site.
The silence shields the slumbering mortals
Whilst stealthy creatures move in hidden portals.

My special view is really due
To my pair of binoculars owned but by a few.
On my podium I stand with poise,
In case I hear the slightest noise.

The moon lights up the scenery,
Bright stars shine to cheer me.
Very little stirs below,
Except the hedgehog which is rather slow.

Suddenly, my lens directs me
To something very tasty.
At once I take off in gracious style,
And fly for almost half a mile.

My target scampers out of sight,
But too late – I grab a bite.
My prey is firmly in my claws,
As I fly out across the moors.

An owl has an extraordinary life.
Sometimes it's full of strife.
But overall it's full of a thrill
As I descend to make a kill.

My binoculars have magic powers.
I perch aloft and watch for hours.
My hoot disturbs the still of night,
It might even give some a fright.

Sadly, though, it may seem to be,
Other creatures provide for me.
The skill of hunting still, I relish.
Without it, I most certainly would perish.

Muriel Garcia – December 2014